LOVE AND CRUSH

LOVE

AND

CRUSH

POEMS BY

Barry Wallenstein

PERSEA BOOKS New York

for Daniel and Jessica

Poems in this collection have appeared in:

Huron Review, Encore, Connections, Poets On: Surviving, Manhattan Poetry Review, The Connecticut Poetry Review, The Third Eye, The Croton Review, Sub Rosa, Beloit Poetry Journal, Jewish Chronicle: Literary Supplement, The Pen, Talus, Outloud, Pembroke Magazine, 10th Decade, Prospect Review, Antigonish Review, Rialto, Ploughshares.

For information, address the publisher:

Persea Books
60 Madison Avenue
New York, N.Y. 10010

Library of Congress Cataloging-in-Publication Data

Wallenstein, Barry.
    Love and crush : poems / by Barry Wallenstein.
      p.   cm.
    ISBN 0-89255-158-5
    I. Title.
    PS3573.A4345L68   1991
    811'.54—dc20
                                  90-24270
                                      CIP

CONTENTS

There's a little secret that Barry Wallenstein knows. Nothing out of the ordinary—just that everyday life is surreal, and that the wildest imagination wells up casually, out of common experience. And oh yes, that the hidden human yearnings around us are dangerously seductive:

> In some people's cages
> you can see a smile so rare
> you'd want to be there
> right inside forever
> share that smile
> and behind the owner's back
> live the life of the cage.
>
> Once at a friend's house
> I saw a smile was on fire;
> it melted the bars and took us in.
> In each other's eyes—stillness.
> We saw flesh softening
> but we didn't stay long
> we had to rush out of
> away from
> that terrible lure.
>
> ("Cages")

Inside the world's open secrets there's the teasing sense of an "answer" that's forever slipping out of reach. It presents itself in familiar-seeming images whose surface meanings taunt us into free-floating dread and sadness: "Death the jaded jockey"; the nightmares of "tens of thousands of 4-year olds"; the voice of the beloved, "carefree, built on cares." Joy is given its rightful due, but the power of fear and of what Poe called "the conqueror worm" is never out of sight. The mixture of life-ecstasy and the taste of dust and ashes is most dramatic in "A Love Sequence: Summer and Fall."

These are poems of the inward normal life. They speak of married love and of passion outside marriage, of the mystery of the child still developing in the womb, of the interlocking yet separate worlds of children and parents, of drastic illness and the gathering darkness.

The language, always intimately confiding, moves readily between easy colloquial speech, or even street talk, and formal elegance. Thus, "Living the Life" begins:

> I just peed
> and there wasn't any blood—

and ends:

> I go in a house
> where the quietest rooms hum with
> the planning of some
> hypothetical forward action
> and I go out in the air
> and its the same thing
> some days

Love and Crush is a pure distillation, vivid, buoyant, and serious. What it distills is the whole psyche of an illusionless dreamer: a man of our present moment, very American yet a blood-brother to modern Mediterranean poets as well.

—M. L. Rosenthal

I

GOING ON

Summertime is at the eventide,
and I am released and struck now
by the slow effort which shows
as you rise and walk from there to here.
Late in the day for you
and therefore for us all.

Tomorrow afternoon all the children
with imagination
will bolt upright
and sensing the full sway
of the great years
of lust and scrounging—
will shiver at the power in the old folks
and feel their own bones turn
the spinning hoop
            as they wish
            rush through
the gathering grace of—
            going on.

LOVE AND CRUSH

All the life we love
leaves soon to feed
some other life
other love.

Thus the vigilance of the dinner hour:

The inchworm, thriving on leaves,
defoliates at times and is off;
the beetle, the aphid— that crowd—
threaten every berry bush, every fruit tree;
the woodworm, devious
feels like, looks like
its own meal (crushed pulp)
and the ants all over
swarming by the tree root
will spread out
and draw the eye from the tree.

The centuries brood round the table.
No need to crush or rush
this balanced diet
as we, provender, make our way.

DREAMING OF LIONS

Last night the lions governed:
two scowling cubs with small beards
buckled the grass
waist high and unfamiliar,
while an old one
leaning back on his haunches, unthreatening,
stared deeply into my eyes.

Through this fog of grass
the lions prowled
around a tight flock
of spotted hens.
Not one soft feather was ruffled,
but the eyes and heads of these birds
made an excitement
in front of the large cats
confusing my view.

I couldn't decide
where I sympathized.
The lions were so beautiful, slim
and serious and the hens so excited
and mystified.
They never expected lions,
and even in their midst
they weren't fully aware.

Then the lions were forward.
No grief.
And I was in the wild
grass grey-brown and wheat
and all those whiskers,
relaxing with the hungry prowlers;
no one in a hurry to eat.

ALREADY

Beneath mother's tent
there swims a developing youth movement
lately from the land of dreams
soon to become a riot
and already
my mysterious fish
you have joined me
in the inbetween land.

We are both hurtling back
               you from
               me to
that place you've already forgotten
that place I've heard talk of.

Little ripple
out of this solemn mood
I call to you.

NOT YET THE CHILD

Baby
in the amniotic dream
circles and bumps:
no papers, prints on record
nothing yet
in the eyes of the law.
My eyes are wild.

This fish without a name
carries the light
we cannot yet read by.

FOUR WEEKS TO BIRTH

Our genes are hiding
in the belly of a fish
in the skin of a belly
in the belly of a fish
floating glyphs
micro-hints of dancing ghosts.
So much to come to life
all at once!
A resurrection of
a history of laugh-lines, hair-lines
birthdays.

Grandpa's to come back
carrying what item
what promise of his esteem?
And the others nudge forward
through the hordes, toward our love.

Hilarious mayhem in the blood
with you now on your way.

FROM THE EGG

Under the wilderness of fluorescent light
a child is seen needing,
creeping across the floor,
mightily knocking against a table leg,
a high chair and his own blocks.
This is the child of the blood
of the man who misses him
far away.

Far away and under fire
the battle rages, works its way down
arms over arms, heads unlike themselves
in the fierce bed of the city.

The child crawls from beneath the glare
and looks back, rubs his face,
and stands up above the childhood litter.
He marches forth as he knows the way
sees the man and clears the field.

Face to face
they assume the same age:
identical memories.

(egg)

GHOSTS

Yes, I'm one of them,
a shade up from some past life,
one of many, visiting.
Tonight you ask
am I an early or late emanation?

You hold me closely
as I pass among
those prior kickers
drunk and untied
fading from current ills
lingering in distant miasma and
rising again
through the centuries, ribboning.

And you persist:
might I be a final version
as you loosen your hold?
Each time when I emerge through the elements,
each time enthralled,
I'm brought to earth by questions
prickling my ears
teasing my touch
making me doubt my new formed self.

THE JEWELED MOTHS

It isn't funny any more
always being drawn to the birthday month
the mouth of spring
my own throat's tightness;
it isn't worth rerunning the tape.

I'd rather linger here
amid these jewels
I call the last moths of summer,
a living frieze.

I love these silky antennae
and wax wings that shed no powder
but have the power to still the racket.
I love these moments
beyond the seasons.

So when you call me
to set the date,
to push my hands into muck,
into some problem needs solving,
I'll pass as never before
and turn to my moths
as they are.

GROWING INWARD

How many nights in the blood lily
before the lily dies?

An offending Adam,
felled by a root, crawls
belly low from rose to rose,
from budding iris to browning lilac,
from columbine to columbine.
He could afflict the entire garden
had he gall enough and time.

But he's entered as a guest
in this universe of stems,
an innocent, going forward.
The grasses peel away
as his fingers crush them
and he goes in deeper
to where the sap is quickest
below the pollen, into the tender shoots.

He lies within the shoots
so slenderized and snug.
No one passing near will see him
or notice a flower here, fattened slightly,
or a root there, with a bulge.
Nor will anyone hear the muffled singing
thinned to the highest pitch.
Some, though, might feel the garden quivering,
exhaling odors unfamiliar and rich.

Still, how long can he live there
before the blooms fall around his intruding love?

TO THE CITY FROM THE COUNTRY

After pulling on nothing but weeds
for three months,
sopping up clover
in the piney woods,
I descend into the city

to yank a chain
which lifts a lid
releasing tons of garbage
down a long chute
and into the river

> (into the sea:
> each evening, before the poison rain,
> the detritus of the city becomes my
> charge).

There is a blessed balance
in all this tugging,
the fist on the pull cord,
white knuckles and the release.

Even if I lose my concentration
I feel my time here,
as in the woods,
is all I have.

> (Stitch by stitch:
> glory be to the free fall
> and after.)

LATE SEPTEMBER MORN

On this hill
the colors are changing early
everyone says.
No, late, the leaves say,
hurry.

BEAUTIFUL THINGS

The cicada in Spring,
azalea dark pink and the fragrant
lilac, swans on the lake
and the lightest breeze—
the lake dries
and the subject looks less cheery.
That tweak in her eye is a cinder.

Scratch the rusted shovel
'till the nails break:
bleeding, dig to where shines
each man's nightmare skull,
the deep unbothered eyes.
Bend over and mouth
the sockets, the grains of the bone.

Ah sunflower!
This is the place you don't dare die.

LIKE CHALK

Everywhere I looked one day
there zoomed this bluebird

not blue as any bird
I'd ever seen

not blue as any bird
ought to be

more like light blue
like chalk used for coloring
birds on blackboards.

The wings blur
almost white blue
the eraser dusts blue and white:
the child's jacket
and his palms too
all chalky.

Everyone in the room watches him
slowly drawing a bird
with light blue, light sky blue
chalk and
the color smudges out of the outline.

Even the class of children sprawl
like silk.

ALL THE WONDERFUL THINGS

My father arrived atop
the most beautiful horse;
the bridle was silver tipped and soft,
and at the ends of the bit
two diamonds glistened and—
and the sparks went
all the way into his hands
so when he dismounted
and took my hands
there was a spark of course
that had nothing to do with the horse.

We walked in a field
and gabbed and barked into the night,
heedless of clouds that covered the stars.

Even after he went off,
without the horse this time,
I kept on with our talk
about my views of the city
and his feelings about the city
and all that's lost out there
and how we both felt about that
and on and on and on.

MOTHER

My mother was born
inside an angel cake
did well
to dwell
in the darkness,
but, pressured,
she ate herself out
into the light.
Thus
I was born.

So, for some years
we both, pleased, ignored shadows
and never each other.
I don't remember just how long.
But one day
on a subway platform
I ran from her hand
up the steps & through the streets.
I was very fleet & confused
so I wasn't caught
until out of breath & crying
she reached me properly,
took me home, gently.

I became a flame unto myself
and that too spread.
I tried to set the house afire.

The help I received
was the help I called for;
I'd call out still
but for the shields
and the shields of fortune.

Some day mother will sit
within an angel choir,

some days in fine voice,
on others, a shrinking violet.
Given a cloudless day,
she may look down on me
looking up her way,
my eyes clear and moistened
by her warm feathers,
the bright sight of her wings.

THE IRON BOLT

I failed myself
I'd like to think—
fault-finding against
a man not nearby,
chiseling away the fat,
showing how meagre the character,
me sitting on a comfortable wicker couch
hammering away.
How often can that happen
before I'm nailed down?

Just yesterday I was puttering
around in my cellar
where it's damp, three-quarters mud,
with unidentified molds on the handles
of paint cans heavy with rust
and the ceiling so low
that when I stand,
even I, a short one,
clang my head against the waterpipes
wet with humidity.

But the truth is I love it down there
doing things
long after there's nothing to do.
I sat down near the boiler
fuzzy with age
and I noticed the leak
I'd almost worried about
had stopped on its own.

On the damp ground I saw an old bolt,
moved it about six inches
and rose up, struck with the thought,
never far from me, that
this place—its iron bolt—
presents an odd package
with designs.

II

SUGAR

The table in the park
is set for five.
The odd person is everyone
else's favorite—a sport, a duke,
sometimes a dandy.
They'd eat him if he had more stamina;
he'd leave them if there were a rodeo
in town
or a great comedian.

But there is no one in town tonight
except himself
and his four friends.
He didn't have to scratch around
for them,
they've been his for years.

Under the shade
of a cool summer evening
these old feelings
are driving his life.

NOT DECADENCE

It's true
as with a teasing straw
we draw each other's blood
and lie backwards or forwards for pleasure.

Yet we are not the.true devils.
Whether eating by the side of an old highway
out of sight of the cars
or up high
in a city skyscraper
we are five or six for dinner.

If a fly buzzes past we ignore it.
If a subject comes up
we cover our ears.

No, it's not grave simplicity.
It's arms and legs gaining in excess,
becoming weak, then strong,
stronger in the mind than iron.

THE UNINVITED FRIEND

No no no   no need to come along
to the party—everyone obvious
high and attentive
where the juggling act
blindfolded against the company
would only tire you out
take you from your pleasure
staring at Tony
who's weakened lately
and is spinning less wondrous webs.

No need to dress
you're uninvited
and when you ask
what went on out there
don't look over my shoulder
look into my talking face
telling the truth
with all the edges you enjoy.
When I'm done I'll ask about your spider
and your time.

VISITING

My head unscrews itself
and floats off into the next room
where, careless of gravity, it gracefully
ascends to the ceiling.

There it hangs out in a high corner
ears tucked against the right angle
eyes look down on a man
asleep on a large bed
miserable
pinched eyes and occasional twitches.
Only the jaw is relaxed—mouth agape:
some drugged spittle dries white
on the upper lip.

I want to return to my body
in the other room.
What made leave that form I know?
It too can lie down, die, dim again
and light up springing.
Everything, in fact, that goes on here
can take place there as well.

MACABRE

If there's any taste left in the cat's mouth
after chewing on you
my 3-months, 2-days dead dear friend
then . . .

(how I knelt & keened
over your body
—the two of us
in a suburban wilderness.
I knew no one could hear me
so I let out
what I'd held back
all the years of your life.
Then my voice failed
and I simply sat still,
stared and finally thought about
you as a body.

But soon the body became
a different attraction,
a host for busy strangers so small
and pesky—so different from you
in life or even myself.
After having stayed through chill,
damp and the acrid air,
I drew back to under the maple
we loved.
I rested, never losing sight of you
and regained my anger)

. . . that cat can lick its lips
and nip my arms,
numb as they've been
these 3 months and nearly 3 days.

IN THE MIDDLE OF THE STORY

So—where's the boss's daughter—
please, where is that tough luck
child of privilege
last seen with you, bruiser?
Did you think you'd protect her,
you, a hireling
come in riding,
still a stranger to the town?

The old man's a deep fixer—
kept her in the dark—
keeps all of us here in the dark;
a regular wheel of fortune
he is
and you thought you could steal—what—
shed some light
and come out better?
Better tell
for the old man's getting mighty tired
and if he falls asleep
and has that vision,
he'll wake in a rage
and cut you—
cut you to strips
of no longer important
human meat.

THE GYPSIES

park their cars in certain places
they shouldn't,
like twenty feet behind my house.
they know it's against the law
and knowing that makes them bolder.
hours pass with little or no movement
as we try to live our normal lives
three meals—T.V.
mending holes—sweeping up.
we avoid obvious changes,
sudden moves to the door or phone.
during the time of their parking
we still hold each other but shyly.

not them!
we have to drag junior from the window.
he knows about the birds and bees of course
but not about the swamps and alligators.
there is no explaining
what we saw last night,
nearly popped the lenses
from the field glasses
we had to hide
(wouldn't want them to see us looking).
they move so slowly.
they arrive in three—sometimes five—
cars at a time
all repainted dark
and it seems hours from when they pull in
to when they step out from those cars.

they poke about fully dressed,
partially dressed, or as nature made them.
in the background their cars sit
looking like dull stones brightened by
streamers and feathers
stuck randomly to the mirrors
visors and back bumpers.

in the evening their sounds drift over
and there is always music.
they mill about in small clusters,
a few alone.
we occupy three windows, amazed.
they hardly ever look this way
except at dusk when
three or four of them will suddenly separate
from the piebald pack
and comically shake fists
in this direction,
not at any one of us,
more or less at the foundation of the house.
then they turn away and forget
what they were thinking.

tomorrow half the group
—more smiles than frowns—
will gather near one man,
an old greybeard pointing directions,
and by evening the whole tribe
will satisfy itself in formation
and the next day,
leaving a little garbage behind,
they'll disappear.

JEW IN DISGUISE

I wear a brown shirt
and my pants are really leather.
The shirt is soft, simply made
simply fine
with buttons & skin underneath
which breaks into a rash
when I worry
or blisters when I'm burned.

A year ago the brownshirts
were a danger,
ghastly on the land.
Who would want to know them
in those days?
Who could know what they meant
marching
that way—I remember.
Who would face them
above their collars
or decline
their determined eyes?

They did their damage.
Then they came home
and changed.

I wear a brown shirt.
Once a week I send it out
and wear another.
This is a dream I freeze.
I thaw it—freeze it
and thaw it out
over & over.

CAGES

In some people's cages
you can see a smile so rare
you'd want to be there
right inside forever
share that smile
and behind the owner's back
live the life of the cage.

Once at a friend's house
I saw a smile was on fire;
it melted the bars and took us in.
In each other's eyes—stillness.
We saw flesh softening
but we didn't stay long
we had to rush out of
away from
that terrible lure.

TWO 14-YEAR-OLDS TALKING FROM CITY JAIL

In the cold gray ward
bothered by no one finally
the boy and girl sit
on two separate cots
—she visiting, he entertaining:

> when I get outa here
> I'm going to Canada
> once there I'll do one last job
> —enough to buy a house
> and a car
> and some easy time

and she said

> hey, check you out

and he talked past that

> I'll even go fishing
> —any day man, I mean
> what the shit
> I've been takin' it
> all this time

(he shows the half-starved waif
his bruises, where they nearly
flayed the skin off his back)

> yeah! I'm gonna get up there

and she, half a tear caught
in the corner of her lips
said

> hey, check you out

and he drew on his cigarette hard
and didn't say anything
for a long while
and then he said

      maybe after I get out
      after I serve this time
      before I head North
      I'll see Sharon one more time
      yeah, I'll see Sharon again—
      check that out sweet stuff
      what d'ya think?

well (she said) well . . .
and laughed softly with no meanness
and she nodded her head
with a sad tick
and didn't say anything else.

And for the first time
since she was let in
he stood up
and with a bow, a smile and a wink
he took his cigarette all the way in
to his mouth
and rounding his broken lips
blew smoke rings out
and with his tongue
he flicked the butt
onto the cement floor
and with just the toe of his shoe
he ground it out.

She sat there
pulling a loose thread
from her sleeve.

Finally she got up
and stood for a last hug.

       Listen
       don't worry about me
       who loses things anyway
       it's a joke anyway

       if you're inside, you're inside
       and if you're on the outside
       that's just another chance.

A PARANOID SCOT FREE

There's a drowning in my imagination
god damn
and I want to dam it up
staunch its possibility.

There's a hanging in my mind.
Cut it, I should get a scissors
sharp enough to quickly clip
a harmless cord.

There's a car accident.
On the way to a hospital
where I'm visiting myself
bandaged from toe to crown
we run off the road.

There's a bludgeoning—freeing,
a twisting of the knife—a dream,
a spot of typhoid—disappearing,
a deep languor—savored,
a hammock in the yard,
a game of chess in winter
by a safe fire

a safe american family.

III

THE POWER OF PRAYER

---

*It was the day the dust refused to desist
swirling blinding the one-eyed
and the two-eyed alike.
No one in the town had prayed
for anything like this.
Someone outside the town surely must have.*

LIVING THE LIFE

I just peed
and there wasn't any blood

that doesn't make any difference—
I'm just as good as
claudia, susan or the man
they call nick the final blaster

what floats by on the calm surface
need not be shot at
but if it happens
and the duck (in pieces) dies
who's going to make the front pages
". . . shot for resisting . . ."
something

these are the times violence
kisses itself all over
there is not enough gas in the ground
to suck up

I go in a house
where the quietest rooms hum with
the planning of some
hypothetical forward action
and I go out in the air
and it's the same thing
some days

WORLD'S END CAFE

Where do the hunted, the sadly haunted
run to right before
they're called out
made to stand on some line
and tell truths about
why they ran
and what they were doing
either sitting around (dodgy eyed)
or pacing back and forth
in a closed room (buttons and switches)
with no windows overlooking the sea.

No view at all
for those bent over
no freshening sea breezes
on those necks, those dirty dirty necks
and no matter how alive the mind
how ready the wit
—agile fingers
scratching ass
—the eyes made up
to look younger,
they remain on line and taking questions.

Still, they don't give in.
They ooze what they ooze
slaving for the trials
slithering from the trials
into silence and the dark cells.
Theirs is the dream of running always
out of the tight room, out of the hour
to some time long ago
or ahead to where the line doesn't end.

No holiday light left
in those still beautiful human eyes.

SOME TOWNS; EVEN CITIES

Through some towns
Death the jaded jockey
presses more tightly
on his spurs.
The horse literally flies.
Eyes shut rather then behold
such misrule.
Children become matches,
little sulphur heads
struck by a design.

(The local gentry, the polite ones,
invite The Monster for dinner.
They let him rest in their midst.
They arm him for battle.
And The Monster, having eaten well,
eats them too.)

The hamlet, the village,
even the city—some cities,
know that when it feels bad,
soon, it's going to smell bad.
IT—the clouds smile down
and gather quickly:
they expel some new hardware
no ordinary cloud could fathom.
There is no boasting in the heavens
at such times.

NIGHTMARES OF THE VERY YOUNG

Every minute, each tick of the night
all over the world,
tens of thousands of 4-year-olds
are shocked loose from dreaming:
hot and squinched, they lie
not cute,
their small teeth grinding.

Some free spirits pitch their screams
high and loud enough
to crack even the glassy eyes
of the night spectres.

Others, though, stifle their cries;
savvy, they dare not call out
for fear they'll disturb and quicken
what plunges through the darkness
towards their beds.

Thus they grip themselves around
and soon squeeze back into the dream
where, wriggling there, they're safer
thrashed and tied
than bashed and shamed above.

IN THE COUNTRY

Two first cousins
pressed up close together
in a one-room shanty, pushing
as much to get close to the stove
as to that feeling they both learned about
on the way to the stove.
For a minute they were embarrassed.
They got warmer through the year.

Into the tiny room is born a tiny infant boy,
slow from the start
but a sticker.
Now it's this boy who stands out in the market.
He steals the light from
the motley groups of wooden-toothed
cousins who jibe, smoke and chew around him.

WHAT SELF DESTRUCTS

Is a thick field of grass
any more a godsend
on account of the lush evidence
than the thin, parched plot
of dying grass?

I no longer know.

Maybe the grasses, if they could raise voices,
would bless the browning over,
the frozen rest beneath the snow.

Nations veer towards . . . what?
One by one or in multiples
they play giddy in the sand.
One child, a curly angel,
buries his little sister;
then it's his turn to get cozy
underboard. By evening both are covered
up to their necks.

What about the tide and
the enlarging shadow all along the beach?

THE WAR

I knew
this would be the last thing done on earth.
I sensed, I knew too that too soon
I'd die.

Weeks before the war began
I started scrubbing myself—showering
two, three times a day—washing my hands
over and over.
I was clean before
                    hop
but then I knew
into the cleanest creases
of my worried skin
something was up and soon to be over.

                    hop hop
Now I'm a frog
grounded beneath twisted
already rusted, pitted steel.
Each time the blasts thunder
(and the broiling heat)
I dive into whatever mud's left,
flick my tongue at whatever flies,
some mite fallen off its wing
and swallow.
No joy in the poisoned meal.

My spots have been gone for hours.
I'm sticky skin drying
and blind all of a sudden.

AT GROUND ZERO

Far outside the warren
where rabbits cuddle around their paws
and a myriad of insects tick and intuit
the chemical change,
a rumbling crash comes down.
A tower falls, from old age,
earthquake or detonation?
Some terrible spreading timbre
no one knows.

Inside, where they breathe,
close to the animals,
hear the tiniest sweetest coos and sighs
and the hard rubbings of fur.
But step back from the creatures
and your antique mouth
is dropped by the booms
constant and nearing
old age falling down
hearts stopped
by the giant flares
coming at last to the heart,
to the snug places
where even toward the final hour
fresh droppings flavor the soil.

EMPIRE

Standing, bent at the waist,
I was arranging my money,
making little piles of coins,
stacks of bills.
Imagine Empire—
roads leading around the sterling towers,
lakes reflecting mountains of bills.
One might think it amusing
to knock over the table
and watch the tiny people
topple each other
in the search for true currency.

In the middle of that joke
I caught the shadow
of a huge man wielding a hammer
about to aim a blow at my head.
So I whirled around
and tightly grabbed this fiend
and squeezed and wrapped my arms
around his middle
& squeezed even harder
& his lower half bubbled out
& his top half bubbled out
and soon he looked like
a squeezed bar-bell
all top and bottom
—no middle.

His hammer fell
and it was sponge too.

MACHINES

There is no machine made
that has not been put to use,
cranked up, plugged in
or triggered.
All apparatus long for deliverance
from inaction.

The spring tension tight
must uncoil. "Did a boy
ever make a snowball
he didn't throw?"

From the arrow to the sling,
the boomerang to the laser,
the target's wish
has its wish
trembling the oceans
trembling the skies.

FASTER

Everything rests on faster:
the finger race
to litter space
faster than thy neighbor;
the foot race to the verge.

As long as fuel holds out
people will gather in groups
and figure accelerations
for working & shaking the hands
& killing & kidding & kindling
clutching & running downhill
even in bonging & the booms go off
in rapid succession
in the bang away blue
blues   deep blue.

IRANGATE

The big man sells guns
to a little man
who pays cash to another little man
who's hung up on the big man, being
a little middle man
a pocket man
a pocket
who buys more guns from the big man
to sell to another little man
who needs to shoot &
otherwise prove himself strong to

folks who eat beans
& would rather water a seed
than be tied backward on a rack, a wheel
that turns the engines in the heart
of that big man & all those
directly plugged into his arse
getting fatter—less little
with every meal, deal

fart.

NEW YORK TO LONDON

The sting bat double back
run away from what's crazy.
Even in your own core
white trembly fingers weave
what no one ever sees,
a frenzied signaling

about whales & waters & currency
& bestiality & water
& children & war again
can never be just war again.
Your hand with its dancing worms
had best strap down.

The sting in the wind
is what you're used to.
Come all this way
to hasten a bet
rest your eyes
& instead it's the eternal city
one more time.
No cause for panic,
your condition is general
& remains stable.

UNHINGED BY THE MEADOW

All along the crushing tide
the ocean channels
the south Devon coast.
It could be cut deeper
and might yet,
but for now, time holding,
the land is as it is
and the sea troubles only
the daring riders or
those in the jaws of insensitive fish.

Above the roar of the waves' hard rub
where striking stones force against themselves,
high ledges relax to farmed meadows,
soft quilts of earthen shades.
Brown are the freshly tilled squares,
veiled and deep green, the framing patches.

On a dry spot, a man lies down
who was never shy;
face pressed to the grass,
he hums into the lushness.
He rolls his right cheek against the blades
and his left reveals the sunlight.
As if taught by that light,
he sees the light exploding,
the sea broiling and swollen,
frenzied at the cliff heights,
carrying over the high land,
up even to his ready boots.
Then this man
who rarely finished a book
feels his meadow rising
above the bluffs of Devon.

BASEBALL

About which I know nothing

except that a hard smash
pulled one way
could fell the first baseman,
or the other way
the man in charge of third.
The second baseman, slim and fixed
on winning one moment,
the next moment may not have a moment
to get out of the way of flying spikes.

Anything can happen in the field
to say nothing of the beanballs
or slippery, lethal spitters.

The advice is, when shagging flies
keep your eye on the ball always
and forever you can stay out late
and never contemplate
dark spheroids
of the night.

THE FIRE

"The fix-it man can't fix *everything*,
no one can—only fire."
                                        —Daniel, 3½ years old

Snow white moth before me
seems all wings, lacelike
with filament thin feelers.
Tonight they fail in the real world,
fragile and in need of heat
they fly into the candle flame.

So too my own life spills toward fire.
My life, my city, state
the whole region of life
crackling, slimy, scorched deeply
finally.

What does a rooster know
pecking near a common fence
the paint flecking from the wood?
My foot against the ground
makes a startling sound
which makes the bird go round
in a fluff of wings.
The colors sunburst red and brown
even the straw on which the rooster struts
is dyed and deeply beautiful.

The moth in flight
the animal in the yard:
as you read
there is no great or grave fire.

IV

LOVE TALK

Now I return to you old boot face.
I tried to get away
before the rough going ran
to miles per hour—wouldn't do
I had to get back to you
no less a person, straighter in fact,
I had to get back to your frown.

When I left you said—get out
and bite whatever shoulder is fair.
I did dive, nearly drowned
into the melee, a wealth of foolish treatment,
but I'm clean, a flip and a whistle.
I'm back to you my cruel cousin.

I can be led to your moods.

HAZARD HEAT

In the hazard heat
I met my love
she met my eyes
and waltzed about my love.

The careful darling!
I've seen her
as a point of light—controlled
me in one room
she in another
scheming with a man
she doesn't even know.

She's careful not
to confuse him
with problems of me
in the next room.

       100 degrees:
       I see a file of fortified men
       sure of my station,
       waiting for her hand
       a rosebud—a fist—
       100 degrees
       in the summertime,
       some things happen
       to warm up and make more
       comfortable the rest of the year.

In the hazard heat
one of us arranges the shoulder
for the other to faint against
and later . . .
we dance.

IN THE HAND OF A PRINCESS

I'll write for you—
you hold me in three fingers
as you would an ordinary pen
but I'm not you know
for you I'm special
my glide would be
—if I had them—
lightning sparks
in your mind
so you love me—smile
at my dulling point
naughty of you to slide me
behind your ear beneath
golden perfumed ringlets
can't write a straight line
(who says that—
your mind or mine?)
then in a pensive frame
you chew my nub—oooh
the length of my life depends
on the thoughtful pressure of your hand
and the teasing bite of your teeth.

THE HANDSOME PRINCE

The Prince surges through brush
to a far side of the garden
where even the deepest weeds
feel the pleasure of his passing
and he never dies.

As far as looks are concerned
he looks something like you
sir.
Would you wear skirts and
spend hours fixing your eyes in a glass?
Still, he does look like you.

As you hulk your way
across the avenue,
and the city chokes you
but fails to slow your charge,
you might reflect your kinship,
rise to kiss the one on your right
and, deaf to the sirens,
bury kisses in the neck to your left.

IN THE BREATH OF THE DRUM

It wasn't her smooth slick bright
sports car
or the yellow tinge 'twixt her teeth
that won my sighs, my spells,
my body one time I say,
nor was it
her healing strokes;
nothing so gentle crossed my mind.
It was her gaze (the long kind)
at my sister looking down
that set me up bright
for what she'd do
between this room and tomorrow.

MACHO MOUTH

She had a splendid fever
        when I took her
says macho mouth.

The little he knows
        she may have feigned fever
some bogus heat
        to keep the grudge off.

Macho teeth grins his way
        around my side of the story.
Tells of her sounds
        tells of his role as star
and how, when the time is right,
        he can be sooo considerate.

She never saw your eyes
        macho pants.
She saw only mirrors
all her life.

PERSONAL PLEA

You don't look like your daddy
you don't look like your daddy

You don't smell like fish
you don't smell like fish

Do you scare?
Were you scared?
Are you scared?

Come out of the closet
dark and crowded
his long coats
her furs
everything shrouded.

(Why did they keep the phone in there?
The ring was so faint
unless you heard it, hiding.)

It's over young man
and you're just tired.

The phone number's changed
and they're gone
and the furs are gone.

It's stuffy, unhealthy in there;
turn around and come out

you original!

FANCY TAKES ME HOME

I call my major pain Fancy.
Fancy took me home to her house,
locked out worries,
kept me in stitches;
I was in knots

       bent over—ague
       bite down—tight torn.
       Muscles felt like nerves in trouble.

How could I understand Fancy?
How could Fancy understand me?

Suddenly she frowned
finding me dazed
light and near to dreaming.
She said
"Wake yourself.
Gather what you need into the circle,
take your medicine
and wait."
I didn't wait long—
cold transport to a new address.

Fancy free now.
It's a short term tenancy
in her house, and up close,
it's nothing but a goddamn shack.

LUCKY MAN

OK—so you're free at your work,
a gentle terror getting ahead—very lucky.
Everyone sharpens up to your face,
no one bothers your time.

The ride home beats the traffic,
you're in a controlled skid.
When the sun gleams off the river,
sunshades glide you safely home.

Home
pure grain gin—lemon
the afternoon's free—every turn's a free turn
the phone's on machine.

        Lucky
        you never skin a shin
        hurt a hair
        or bother moving things aside
        but take care
        if you don't cheat that luck
        it will kiss you back
        and you'll spend all of your
        last ten years
        as some other person's
        sad memory.

ASSURANCE OF ENTRY

When the witch came out of the wall
I waited   astride the chair I was
not comfortable.
How did she know?
Her assurance was as sudden
as her entry through plaster
which healed before she could sit
so close to me I fell aghast
aginst the pillow
forgetting for a minute my sweet pigeon
standing pressed against the white wall
dressed in beige.
The witch wore the black dress.

She promised to be slow
with my friend
and by the end to be a mercy.

She took this pair of arms I know
so white so slim and stretched
them out   the sight far-reaching.
The windows were down
and the curtains drawn:
the silent mouth opened wet and dry.

So much was managed swiftly,
comfortably,
even the alarms were brief and
incidental.
Now amidst these papers and ordinary errands
I wonder about the magic
that sometimes issues from walls
or comes sifting down
from the heavens.

THE AUTOMATIC FLYING BED

When my shoe comes off fast
it hits the competition like magic.
The others in disarray, turn away.
We win the bed everytime.

Can it bring back even you,
the one we call
last year's obsession,
now drifting, grave and remote

not a mile ahead of the soft sailing
magnetic bed?
You, of questioned fame,
a flame of red—my squeeze—
may be swept to us, heart and head.

WHO SHOULD?

Her anger tightens, relaxes,
pistons, age-old and wearing.
A fury
inflames her already great fatigue.
She languishes in the gut of her own desire.

Who should wake her up
or calm her down?
Her father who strung the bow
and stirred the soup she is?
Or the lover new on the scene
who may do wonders touching even
through her veil, her twitching sleep?

If I should say, Bliss
let's fit that larger painting near
the door
into the smaller one over there,
you'd likely say
when?
or turn around to me and say
when's dinner?

Then we'd, hungry, disappear
from each other
for an hour,
you thinking about getting ready,
feeding the others,
and of the larger canvas:

    still sunset on the water
    grey tide and the declining yachts.

I'd think about the smaller painting
facing the wall:

    the abstract in yellows and reds
    burning up the moisture
    in the air.

Neither of us doubts the trick:
the smaller disobeying the rules,
accepting without pain or breaking
the larger world of factual water.

Neither of us knows just where,
within the frame,
the boats can resurrect
and the frozen sea send out ripples
to the margin.

A LOVE SEQUENCE: SUMMER AND FALL

primarily in the voice of a young woman from Turkey re-
siding in New York. The poems in her lover's voice are in
italics.

I Met This Guy—5/20

(bir Turk kizi yasli bir Yankee ile tanisir)

He came over so dark,
his face part of a larger shadow:
musty rippling silk.
I could have reached over
and, as smart fingers know braille,
shaped a smile there
as fast as I wanted.

I wasn't sure what I wanted.
before allowing my
what? self/love
to be unblocked.
I can block it again or later,
no matter.

Some nights I can sail away
on such currents of light air.
The parachute gliding upward:
a Spaniard, a medical man
on one cloud; on another,
two brothers, German,
light as new feathers.
We laugh with the tickles
and we talk and everything else.

Some days—
like last night,
I settle for the heavier air,
his hugs.
What else am I to do with them
but take them
and give them back as long as he is here.

The Call

How many times in this family rain
have I wanted a sudden shelter,
the phone to ring,
a blanket of pines
12 feet above my head
and growing up thick 50, 60 feet.
No rain then would get through.

But the heedless rain comes down.
The wish for shelter,
confused under this flood of water,
turns luminous and dies.

As the phone takes on the color and shape
of a rock,
igneous and nearly beautiful,
the rain itself begins to glow.

A Date In Spring

Outside the arc of comfort close,
snug forms and the front door bolted,
there's downtown
and a place I know, so open,
so derelict, the calls from a room
are like flowers closing in gentle rain.

I'll go there through
the checked and cracked foyer;
the last person who smiled there
was carried away in a fever.

I won't let the smile out
till after.

Our People: Separate

All the other people we love,
my sisters, Dilan,
and all the great players I've loved
and the lesser ones too
he's never met:
beautiful stacks of cards
he's never touched, seen
or heard me talk about.

And his people,
best unseen,
creep into my corners
and make sounds sometimes
I could shake a stick at.
Other times they make me relax
and imagine they are no worse
than any other sounds
a life has to put up with.

6/19

In this city
I'm not a fish out of water,
for I'm breathing, yes, but
it's hard to explain:
there is this yuppie garden

with all sorts of rich flowers,
and they are not my flowers.
No one I know owns them,
but I love one, even the bush,
the lilac.
I don't love it too much.
I could have it home in winter
or I could simply recall it
or one like it.
This is not my city, but here I am.

6/21

What does he mean when he says
I'm in my sin?
An American expression?
Must be his gin
makes him slip slide every time:
walking out of the room—bang
he falls and I'm not there.
    I'd rather drive around the city
    or sit up high
    above Central Park at 11 a.m.
    looking out from a borrowed room
    with you
he says.
He says this to me
in a cushioned bar
in New York City
at 2 a.m.

6/22

Some day he will ask
"So, where am I in you?"
(I've heard him think this already.)

Well, I'll say,
"Is this about sex
or metaphysics?"
He'll just so brave look blank.
I'll let a minute go by.
"No, I'm teasing," I'll say—
"you're in my ear."

Stolen Figs

I was younger then
and a real rebel.
All the solemn rituals,
roles the orthodox play
(so good, yes, really good people),
I couldn't abide.
Slyly, in fasting time,
I went to the garden
and with my friend, we ate the figs.

Lately something strange has happened.
A guy I know and I
stole a special fig to share.
No matter how we bit it,
how deeply we tasted it,
wetting our mouths, fingers,
our chins glistening,
it wouldn't go down,
we couldn't swallow.
It wanted nothing of our insides.

We can't give the fruit back.
It's ours for now, for taste
and what it yields.
This fig might turn into an idea,
one we might chew on.

The Phone

Telephone?
I prefer the old-fashioned ones, black
with rotary dials,
yet I live with the new kind—
touch tone and it takes his messages.

Sometimes I'd like to rip it out
and walk outside in front of my house
and in the sand draw a circle
and place the nuisance in the center,
raking my bare footprints
as I back out.
Then I'd smile at new friends.
We wouldn't dance around the circle for long.
We'd walk out into the country
for a while.

7/10

He's nervy,
speaking through my voice
while enjoying both sunshine and shade
on the same safe street.
Is he hiding behind that laughing tree?
No. He couldn't be further away.

A stranger approaches me on the street
with a rose, let's say, or a message
from someone back home.
I'll accept the message or the rose
with a smile and a direct gaze

but no matter what we'll say,
he'll stay a stranger.
How can you get close

to someone on the street?
You have to have a reason.

> I have no reason tonight
> he's out of sight
> he thinks I'm in sight
> and he's not even ¼ right.

He's that stranger now
and his hands, strong enough when close,
won't stretch far enough
to offer a rose,
and he'll never carry messages
from anyone back home
or even near by to me.

In My Own Voice

Now it's me
caught beneath the lightning wheel
on an open field
in mid July
on some absent person's
private property.
If he knew, he'd care just a little
and continue talking into his hands.

I will not speak in my lover's voice
for a while though I hear it still
resting inside my mouth
whispering for my tongue to be itself.
It is. And I'm not worried.

Her voice
is violet light,
carefree, built on cares
carefully stacked in a corner

under cover—cares rich enough to eat.
And when she speaks
it's all those light words.

I'm older and so serious.
I write things down.
One time I even wrote her name
15 times in rows
5 rows
3 careful spellings of her name
in each row
then one sentence at the end
having nothing to do with us
to break the spell.

My seriousness may be worn in summer;
around her neck I'll sparkle dark
large garnets—a strand falling
halfway to her waist
catching the light every which way.
I can see her touching them,
pretending absent mindedness,
my gift to her
in my own voice
fired by the lightning wheel
that spins above our doubled head.

The Wave I Know

There was a wave I loved
when I was a young girl.
I never saw it, but I knew.

Our waters were too calm,
but I didn't mind while
wishing for something else.

Now I'm older
and if the camera on that dolly
were to move backwards,
let's say, 40 meters,
I'd be seen engulfed and happily
spitting water from my wave.

Shapeless,
it has no pride in its power.
The whorl upward
is no greater than its shingled stride
backwards, as it rushes to its mother.

Is it satisfied?
Am I?
The foamy bubbles tickling my toes
say maybe yes;
the retreating sounds of the sea
say that too.

7/22

He combs my hair
on rare mornings in summer,
rare and easy to take.

I think now, a day after the last time,
maybe I wasn't all there.
It was lovely—yes,
but a head should be more awake
under such a practiced comb
lightly sliding through.

Looking back, I must have been half asleep.
The combing out of those few knots
at the back near my neck

could have gone on a few minutes longer.
Those wouldn't have been lost,
those few minutes.

And the day went by all right
and the night.

7/25

Of the many marks or decorations
on my body,
there are three
I'd like to know more about:
one is round, soft at the center,
brown and shaped like a thumb print
as if someone had pressed that finger
to the outside of my upper thigh.
I've always had it.

The second is new, red,
dear small bruise
close to my life, hidden
and already fading.
I know who did it
and I know when and
I will keep that straight
for weeks to come.

The third is even newer,
this very night.
I won't bother to look for it.
It's that fresh.
We'll see.

8/4

He's still thinking his way
into my head, oblivious that
I've gone out.
So he's more alone up there
then either of us knows.

It's too hot to think.
The truth is I've been out for days,
walking beneath shop awnings,
avoiding the parks,
eating very little.
Yesterday,
leaning my back against a shaded wall,
I had a vision
I wish I could share:
A foreign city
gulls tipping the inlet river
me tugging at his amazement.

If only he'd step out
away from me and into sight.
What is he doing up there
lying on the floor
looking skyward,
as if my head were crystal
as if he were lonely in my head?

Music, Furious and Cold in the Background

Dear N,
imagine
I'm at the North Pole
(couldn't get higher)
freezing, as in the painting,
with glacial winds testing my mood.

Even my eyebrows are swept.
For a moment
I'm confused where to go—
inside the cabin
100 steep feet away
or behind this medium sized rock
where I could, squatting, shelter myself
'till the blizzard passes.
N, do you think it will pass?

My fingers have been numb
for nearly an hour.
I'm not being teased
by the minute
as could be the case in another world.
Were you here, I'd be no safer
and you'd be in deeper trouble.
Your body, even if packed in pillows,
would shiver quickly.
I'd rather the rock
then your frame, stiff as a board.

But what if you arrive with tickets?
YES! and a sled.
Tickets to the South and strong huskies
to pull the sled.
It's not so far after all
to the cabin to pack—
then, to the airport,
Fairbanks, N.Y., a few calls,
and away away.

8/24

I see a funny spot on the wall
with no real shape,
but with my eyes in a mood

I can form a shape
as easily as I can look away.

When I press my face up close
(not too close
don't want a smudge)
it's a man,
someone I know better then the ceiling.
I never think about ceilings.

It's an all right spot up close.
I know it's kind.
When I sit back
it wavers with the movement and
sometimes, in some poor light, it dims.
All that's for fun
or I can be serious.

If I squint a certain way
I can send it out
or draw it in;
I can narrow it to a line.
I can diminish it to a point.

8/27

What can I do with
this man
shrunk in my hand?
He's little good to me
at such a size.
If I tighten into a fist
will he ooze between
each finger
equally,
or would powder remain,
chalky and clean,
in the lines of my palm?

A Dark Day

How relentless the arc you've become:
the heavy club wrapped in a chain
flies towards my head,
and while I know you didn't wish it
and its path doesn't make you smile,
I also know there is nothing you can do
to stop or shift its aim, now.

Yesterday, even in that heavy weather,
I was protected.
All flying objects had your name,
and they were harmless
and large enough for me to ride.

Anger

Now
I
build an anger.
This grudging temper
which feels like light is
brand new,
an ill-chosen spice
in this story's stew.

I must have fallen asleep
in the middle of a central point
in her argument
which was based on some careful words
of mine she missed,
dozing behind my ear.

After

tonight she's out
catching it fine

there will be two minutes time
between that and sleep

not my fault
fully

(if she were writing on this page
she'd say
'tonight he's out—into himself
mature—I like that
but not tonight.)

fault. faults

(I knew a rock one time
so faulty you could climb it
like a ladder.
I did.)

maybe for the best
her best bet

(I advance
while my love plays wild among the briars)

Rain

Now it's raining again.
Will it, luminous, ever
take the place of freedom,
passion in the capital?

The raindrops need not
formulate as prison bars—
again.

The absence of rain
was an illusion
first one, then the other
settled for.

It's easy to stay up all night
in the music,
drinking from the robbers' cup—
unbreakable even in
daylight.

Sadness In Robes—11/2

Hello Sadness
come out from around that door
the barn door
the city steel door
that lock
that hedge
where I see you
but feel you not enough
to make me proper.
Come, sit on my shoulder.

Sadness now
if you're dry or reluctant
I'll wet you with welcome,
wear you for the weight.
I've held you off long enough,
nearly died of the jollies:
nicotine and the like
and the added soul,
a face that could darken glass,
turn coal to diamonds—

some days—water to ice.
She could melt us both, Sadness,
you and me.
Though, on other days, you, coolly,
visit her thoroughly.

Sadness,
I've kept you at bay with lances,
hand sharpened at the tips,
bright pennants dipping,
my ritual of hiding,
pretending all is splendid:
the easy drives
and excited enjoys.
Sadness, I never didn't think of you.

I'm dropping my sharp defenses
I think.
Sadness, you figure
of my drawn out,
soon to die out, speech,
cloak me in your leaden robe,
old, not too clean,
and she'll be free,
skipping as far from you
for a while,
as she is this day,
from me.

POST SEQUENCE DRIFT

The Gaps Between Them

The glass of water between them
did not bar, ban or challenge their
fevered conversation.

But soon the glass shape disappeared
and the water became a serious ocean,
a sexy flow and barren.

This endless gap, pitch and drowning water
sprays up these facts:
he was just a boy
and she a thriving woman;
he a set stone,
she a sailing moon;
she'd taken her veil off
from the East
and he borrowed plenty, but
only in the West;
he showered,
she was bathed.

There were pleasanter gaps too,
like between their front teeth
drawing attention
and contact—again,
as if no oceans
sank ships.

A Break In

I removed the lock from your front door.
I didn't like returning the keys.
Sitting down in front of your desk,
I relaxed a moment
and accidently broke the chair.
Leaning back,
trying to drift myself into you,
I did.

I was an old boy/young woman
sitting at an old desk,
how old, the grains didn't sing.
I slid the small red box,
carved cinnabar from China,
4 inches to my left
and with my fine right hand
I moved some clips off the writing pad,
and was about to . . .
when I heard the little crack
and fell—
wasn't hurt,
sorry about the chair.

Standing in that room, finally
I was still there
still unrecovered—still out of my body
and the view was not strange,
not once did I look behind me
I was that comfortable.

And I'm here—still in your place
—yours or mine?
The rugs are this way
the walls are this way
posters, windows—light.
The lock's off the door
easy entrance—if you were to enter.

Monkey Talk

"Lately," the monkey says
"when I get into bed with
reclining monkeys,
the two I love,
(on different spots on the clock
and in different corners)
each one sleeps
most of the time I'm there.

So I fuss about the cage and swing,
simulating happiness
rung to rung,
and I roll into the tire
hanging from a long cord
and swing around and around
way past dizzy.
When the circling stops,
I try to focus
on the dozing monkeys,
and I fall asleep.

Sometimes, I dream my fingers
are digging beneath their fur, soft,
and hard are the lice I pick out
to quickly chew.

Blues 1

You
catch my breath with your waking

a calf moves closer to its mother
(slumbering)

some brother leaves his home
to bring me what I need.
It doesn't work & I call you back—

Sugar—I call you Sugar

no rest in my slumber
no sugar in my bowl.

Blues 2

Such accidents do happen
dancing: she says
I'm dancing beneath your loving blow
so I stagger

staggered, he says no:
it wasn't a blow
it was a brush—feather light;
I fly round the world for your gold

another time
she tries so hard
to make him well,
it makes her sleepy

more lately
they share their tricks
but never their secrets
set in codes, dark and changing.
They can barely read what they say,
and when they do, they forget.

Broadway Scene, Could Be

She was slim the young lady,
sightless, it seemed.

One day, tapping her delicate stick
across a dangerous broad way,
traffic screaming beneath invisible lights,
meaningless green; thrilling red,
he, a perfect stranger,
with nothing on his mind,
fell out of his way for her.

From five blocks distant,
and as if caught in a fever,
he leapt cars, vaulted trucks,
and kicked aside the city cans
to assist her stick, attend her hand.

She noticed, quickly
how he sweat
and how difficult it was, panting
to make his words come out right.

For him it seemed an endless glide
crossing over to the other side.
Once there,
he pointed her in a safe direction,
and waited.
Suddenly
she lowered her glasses, smiled
and bit his lip.

Then, as if forever,
he lost his sight for a time.

This Quiet Moment

The few I know—so clearly now,
so close, are asleep
and I, cracked in two and miles away
from half myself,
from half this resting, slowly pulsing
population

sit awake
(like the police)
more alone than before,
and I admit their sleepy breathing
ever this gently
in their dreaming:
little sighs—timed zzz zzzz apart.
I walk over and visit one,
just one;
then, in my mind another and another and another,
(that's enough!)
and I bend over to straighten a sheet,
cover a shoulder,
kiss her forehead,
slip beside—.
No invasion; this brief visit in the dark
is over.

Hardly a sound is coming off the street
in New York City—

Part of this quiet is a hummm,
city-deep, continuous,
sinuous. And now a distant siren—.
Police who never sleep
wait like me
for something tight to wake up
and be restless;
someone delightful at the end of the night
to content with,
this one, again.

Conversation(s): An improper slice

dont say anything
just hold me
dont say anything
hold me
i'm sleepy/really

(other voices)
and the first movie was fine
Molly dont ya think?
—I dont remember.
how could you not?
shhhhh—be still, listen:

hold me tight hold me tighter
   —but I want to talk to you
there's nothing to say—it's late and
your words wont make the wheel stop spinning,
the little ball fall on my number
or make me clean the sink.

   —didja hear that?
   shhhhh—look at his mouth
   he's licking his lips; he's crying
   —but did you hear how she loves?
   I'm listening; you keep quiet

—I'll break my wrists on the wheel
—I'll improve.
sure you will and you'll shave twice a day
and remember to bring home extra bacon.
—Yes, I can imagine doing all that.

shhhhh   just hold me;
I have less on. Fade out